# Pocket Prayers *for* Women

# Simple Prayers of *Blessings*

**pil** Publications International, Ltd.

**Author:** Marie D. Jones

**Additional contributors:** Cecil Cole, Elaine Wright Colvin, Elaine Creasman, Christine A. Dallman, June Eaton, Lain Chroust Ehmann, Georgann Gouryeb-Freeman, Barbara Briggs Morrow, Anna Trimiew, Natalie Walker Whitlock, Gary Wilde

**Cover Art:** Shutterstock.com

**Interior Art:** Art Explosion, Getty, Joan Falquet, Shutterstock.com

Copyright © 2014 Publications International, Ltd. All rights reserved. This book may not be reproduced or quoted in whole or in part by any means whatsoever without written permission from:

Louis Weber, CEO
Publications International, Ltd.
7373 North Cicero Avenue
Lincolnwood, Illinois 60712

Permission is never granted for commercial purposes.

ISBN: 978-1-4508-8301-6

Manufactured in China.

8 7 6 5 4 3 2 1

# Giving Thanks

Humans have a deep desire to converse with their Creator. Whether we're happy or sad, thankful or needy, we want to express what's on our minds and in our hearts to God.

*Pocket Prayers for Women: Simple Prayers of Blessings* is a pocket-size devotional that includes prayers about the blessings God bestows upon us, as well as Bible passages and inspirational quotes to help us further express our gratitude to God.

Best of all, *Pocket Prayers for Women: Simple Prayers of Blessings* is small enough to fit in a purse or briefcase, making it easy for you to take advantage of the privilege of talking with God every day.

# God's Perfect Gifts

*Every generous act of giving, with every perfect gift, is from above, coming down from the Father of lights, with whom there is no variation or shadow due to change.*

James 1:17

In your love, Lord, the gifts just keep flowing into my life moment by moment. The new day, the wonders of the season, all the things I take for granted, such as breathing, sipping a mug of hot tea, or enjoying a warm shower—each is a gift from your goodness. As I reflect on your generosity, I'm deeply appreciative for all you've given me.

# The Good Word

*Finally, beloved, whatever is true, whatever is honourable, whatever is just, whatever is pure, whatever is pleasing, whatever is commendable, if there is any excellence and if there is anything worthy of praise, think about these things.*

Philippians 4:8

Lord, in your infinite wisdom you knew we would need instruction for life, and so you placed in your Word the guidelines for living a productive life that brings you glory. Your Word nurtures us body and soul and keeps our minds focused on the beautiful, positive aspects of life. Thank you, Lord, for not leaving us here without a guidebook. We'd be lost without your Word.

# Come Together

*Where two or three are gathered together in my name, there am I in the midst of them.*

Matthew 18:20 KJV

Heavenly Father, we thank you for the traditions that unite our family. We are bound together in love as we take part in the rituals that were begun so long ago. Bless us with your presence as we attend services together, partake of our traditional dinner, and enjoy one another's company. These traditions make family the first priority for the day. They provide our children with security and confirm that we are important as a group. Please keep us close to each other as we gather around you.

# Prayers of Others

*I thank my God every time I remember you, constantly praying with joy in every one of my prayers for all of you.*

Philippians 1:3–4

Thank you for those who pray for me, Father. Thank you for putting me in their hearts and minds. I know that at times people are keeping me in their prayers, and I haven't the faintest clue. It could be my hairdresser, my pastor, or even someone I've just met. Perhaps a checker at the grocery store recalls a bit of conversation we had and now prays for me from time to time. You work in such unusual ways that I never know how it might be happening—I just know that it is so, and I am grateful.

# Promise of Salvation

*I am the way, and the truth,
and the life. No one comes to the Father
except through me.*

John 14:6

Jesus was the fulfillment of God's promise of salvation. His life and death made salvation possible for us. What a glorious, selfless gift! I ponder this blessing every day, and gratitude and joy fill my very being.

*What is a charitable heart?
It is the heart of him
who burns with pity
for all creation.*
—St. Isaac the Syrian

# Daily Reminders

Lord our God,
 You are the great God
You are the creator of life;
You make the regions above
and sustain the earth from which we live.
You are the hunter who hunts for souls.
You are the leader who goes before us.
You are the great mantle which
 covers us.
You are the one whose hands are with
 wounds.
You are the one whose blood is a living
 stream.
Today we say thank you, our God
and come before you in silent praise.

—African prayer

# Ever-Present Lord

*Blessed are those who have not seen
and yet have come to believe.*

John 20:29

Lord, how blessed we are to be able to see you all around us and to sense your presence within us. Even though we can't see you in the same way we might see a friend or a neighbor, we see you in your Word and in all that is good and true in the world around us. Thank you, Lord, for making yourself so available to us.

# Honest Work

*If a man will not work, he shall not eat.*
2 Thessalonians 3:10 NIV

Gracious Father, you are at work day and night on our behalf as you watch over us. We know that work is a noble thing, a necessary part of life, and that we are all fellow workers with you.

We thank you, Lord, for the opportunity for honest labor, and we present ourselves to you as workers who need not be ashamed.

*Work is love made visible.*
—Kahlil Gibran, *The Prophet*

# Growth Rings

O Lord, bless our life stages, for they read like growth rings on a tree: our beginnings and firsts with their excitement, newness, and anxiety; our middles, full of diligence and commitment and, yes, sometimes boredom, but also risk and derring-do; our "nexts," the harvests and reapings, the slowing down and freedom. In your hands this time can be rich and full like an overflowing cup, not a last or a final or an empty or an ending stage at all.

*Just a tiny seed of faith, watered with love, wisdom, and hard work, grows into a majestic tree of blessings.*

# Blessings of Silence

When we fill our days with the noisy blur of constant activity, we miss the gifts and blessings of silence and stillness. Only by purposely taking the time to do nothing can we cultivate the inner wisdom and guidance we seek. In the quiet we renew our connection to the source of inspiration, energy, and enthusiasm. Silence is more than golden. It's essential to a life well lived.

*In silence I kneel in your presence; bow my heart to your wisdom; lift my hands for your mercy. And open my soul to the great gift: I am already held in your arms.*

# Filled with the Spirit

*Be filled with the Spirit, as you sing psalms and hymns and spiritual songs among yourselves, singing and making melody to the Lord in your hearts, giving thanks to God the Father at all times and for everything in the name of our Lord Jesus Christ.*

Ephesians 5:18–20

You don't need to have perfect pitch to sing praises to God. Many worshippers take great comfort in the psalmist's mandate to make a joyful noise to the Lord. Joyful noises from attuned hearts are music to God's ears.

# Offering Comfort

*Let each of you look not to your own interests, but to the interests of others.*
Philippians 2:4

So much need around us, O Lord. Inspire me to care for those who need. Even the smallest gesture is powerful, bringing moments of peace and contentment into circumstances thought hopeless.

*God does not comfort us to make us comfortable only, but to make us comforters.*
—Dr. John Henry Jowett

# Promises Kept

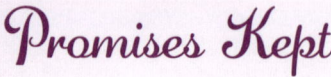

*When God made a promise to Abraham, because he had no one greater by whom to swear, he swore by himself, saying, "I will surely bless you and multiply you." And thus Abraham, having patiently endured, obtained the promise.*

Hebrews 6:13–15

Lord, I have a lot of people in my life who let me down and make promises they don't keep. My greatest blessing is knowing that you will never go back on your promises to me and that I can always turn to you for anything. You never fail to give me what I need and to withhold from me the things that I might think I need but really don't.

Your wisdom guides me in all my ways, and your promise of eternal love is the only true blessing I desire.

> *Blessings aren't always wishes fulfilled and promises kept. Sometimes the greatest blessings come in the form of what we are denied.*

# God's Wondrous Gifts

*For the Lord is good; his steadfast love endures forever, and his faithfulness to all generations.*

Psalm 100:5

Lord, if I were to boil down all the good news in the universe and look to see what I ended up with, there would be the eternal realities of your goodness, your love, and your faithfulness. And in this world, I don't have to look far for them—family, food, shelter, clothing, seasons, tides, sun, moon, stars, life, beauty, truth, salvation. And that's just a sampling, a preview of a much longer list. I'm moved to praise you and to tell you how much I love you back.

# Basis of Faith

*Faith is the root of all blessings. Believe, and you shall be saved; believe, and your needs must be satisfied; believe, and you cannot but be comforted and happy.*
—Jeremy Taylor

Blessings, like miracles, appear only when we believe in them. Faith gives us the eyes with which to see and to believe what we see.

# Spreading the Wealth

*There is great gain in godliness combined with contentment; for we brought nothing into the world, so that we can take nothing out of it; but if we have food and clothing, we will be content with these.*

1 Timothy 6:6–8

Content with just food and clothing? Really, Lord? I'm thankful that you provide for my basic needs, but there's much more on my wish list. This passage makes me realize how much I expect in life. Help me to be thankful for the countless blessings in my life and to always be ready to help others rather than focusing on adding to my own stores. Please guide me, Lord. I'm ready to answer your call to contentment.

# For the Beauty of the Earth

For the beauty of the earth,
　For the glory of the skies;
For the love which from our birth,
Over and around us lies;
Lord of all, to Thee we raise
This, our joyful hymn of praise.
For the joy of human love,
Brother, sister, parent, child;
Friends on Earth and friends above,
For all gentle thoughts and mild;
Lord of all, to Thee we raise
This, our joyful hymn of praise.

—Folliott S. Pierpoint

*With boldness, wonder, and expectation,
I greet you this morning, God of sunrise.*

# Seasons of Life

*They are like trees planted by streams of water, which yield their fruit in its season.*

Psalm 1:3

The older I get, the more aware I am of the seasons of life, Lord. I know that when we draw our energy and resources from your living Word, we can be compared to the trees that thrive near streams of water. The fruit of a young life lived for you may look a bit different than the fruit visible in the lives of older folks, but it all brings you glory. Thank you for supplying your living water through all the seasons of our lives. Without it, we could bear no worthy fruit at all.

# Be Blessed

May you find joy and satisfaction in your family life:
in building a home and setting up a residence—be blessed!
in finding a job and working diligently—be blessed!
in taking care of little ones and making friends in the neighborhood—
be blessed!
in seeking God for all your help and guidance, bringing every care to him, yes, I pray, may you indeed be blessed.

*Count on your family, especially when it comes time to count your blessings.*

# Pay It Forward

*Have unity of spirit, sympathy, love for one another, a tender heart, and a humble mind. Do not repay evil for evil or abuse for abuse; but, on the contrary, repay with a blessing. It is for this that you were called—that you might inherit a blessing.*
1 Peter 3:8–9

Lord, the last thing I want to say to the person who tailgates me in traffic is "Bless you." Oh, but how graciously you've blessed my life, even when I've been the one acting like a jerk. Please help me redirect my focus toward how I've been treated by you. Then I'll be able to draw from your great reservoir of mercy and pay it forward in the form of a blessing instead of a curse.

# Common Things

God give me joy in the common things;
In the dawn that lures, the eve that sings.
In the new grass sparkling after rain,
In the late wind's wild and weird refrain;
In the springtime's spacious field of gold,
In the precious light by winter doled.
God give me joy in the love of friends,
In their dear home talk as summer ends;
In the songs of children, unrestrained;
In the sober wisdom age has gained.
God give me joy in the tasks that press,
In the memories that burn and bless;
In the thought that life has love to spend,
In the faith that God's at journey's end.
God give me hope for each day that springs,
God give me joy in the common things!

—Thomas Curtis Clark

# Everyday Celebrations

My Creator, blessed is your presence. For you and you alone give me power to walk through dark valleys into the light again. You and you alone give me hope when there seems no end to my suffering. You and you alone give me peace when the noise of my life overwhelms me. I ask that you give this same power, hope, and peace to all who know discouragement, that they too may be emboldened and renewed by your everlasting love. Amen.

*If you have something to do, someone to love, and something to hope for, every day becomes a celebration.*

# Love of Any Kind

*Set me as a seal upon your heart,
as a seal upon your arm; for love is strong
as death, passion fierce as the grave.*
Song of Solomon 8:6

Lord, being in love is a magical gift. Everything seems brighter and sharper in focus. My heart soars and my spirit is light as air, and all because of the love of another. But help me to also seek that deeper, more lasting love that comes from truly knowing another, even when the fires of passion become a gentle and steady simmer. Let love always be in my life, no matter what form it comes in. Love of any kind is a magical gift. Thank you, Lord.

# Gifts from Above

Now thank we all our God
with hearts and hands
and voices,
who wondrous things hath done,
in whom this world rejoices;
who, from our mothers' arms,
hath blessed us on our way
with countless gifts of love,
and still is ours today.

—Martin Rinkart, translated
by Catherine Winkworth

*How good it is, Almighty One,
to bask in the warmth of your love.
To know nothing more is required than
this: Receive your good gifts from above.*

# True Wealth

*Give me neither poverty nor riches;
feed me with the food that I need.*

Proverbs 30:8

Lord, as I struggle to balance my budget, I ask myself: What is wealth? Is it having material riches, plenty of food, clothing, a house, and freedom from worry about money? You have taught me, Father, that it is none of these things. True wealth is having work to do. It is being cared for by a loving God. It is enjoying the love of friends and family. You give me all I need or want, Lord. I am the wealthiest of people.

*Wealth is not measured in money and possessions; it is a state of mind.*

# Place of Joy

*Let all who take refuge in you rejoice;
let them ever sing for joy.*

Psalm 5:11

I have often asked myself this question: How do I make my home a place of joy? Now I know—the answer lies with you, O Lord. Like St. Augustine, our hearts are restless until they find their home in you. Life seems steadier, brighter, friendlier, safer. Your presence fills us with music. We make joyful noises when we sing your praises. All thanks to you, precious Lord, for our happy home. I will sing to you as long as I live.

*Joy is the presence of God in our lives,
which brings music to our souls.*

# First God, Then Good

*Happy are the people to whom such blessings fall; happy are the people whose God is the Lord.*

Psalm 144:15

God, how long have I looked outside of myself for the blessings that were waiting all along? How often have I complained to you about life not being the way I wanted it when I already had what I needed to change? I now know that the blessings of prosperity and joy are all an inside job. By turning first to you, dear God, all else is then opened before me. You taught that your Kingdom was within, not without, and yet once we recognized it, we would also see it all around us. Thank you, God.

# God's Guidance

*He will be our guide for ever.*

Psalm 48:14

Thank you, God, that even when I fret, I know without a doubt that you are using my unique, special gifts and talents to their fullest potential. When I get down on myself and am unsure of my abilities, remind me that your commitment to me is lifelong.

*Aim high, believing that God has great things in store for us. Never mind naysayers and "practical" roadblocks, for we are guided by God.*

# Lord of Love

Father, you are a God of love, compassion, and forgiveness. You have shown my family the right way to live. We can count on you to guide us and keep us safe. You boost our confidence and make us better than we are. Lord, we do not deserve your care and attention, but you give them anyway. For this we exalt you forever.

*How much does God love you?*
*He loves you enough to let you go.*
*He loves you enough to let you hit bottom.*
*He loves you enough to let you come back.*
*He loves you so much that he will run to meet you.*
*That's how much God loves you.*
—Ray Pritchard, *The Road Best Traveled*

# True Friendship

Almighty God, of all the things you've created, friendship must be among your favorites. What a joy it is for me to be with my friends, Lord. What encouragement and affirmation I get from them—and what correction if it's needed. That's the beauty of true friendship. It isn't just for here and now. It's forever.

*A true friend is the gift of God, and He only who made hearts can unite them.*

—Robert South

# Unfailing Love

Father, bless me with a wonderful expectation of the things which are coming. With hope for the next life, I will not be discouraged in this one. Please send your spirit to be with me as I learn to trust in your unfailing love. And I pray that I, being rooted and established in love, may have the ability to grasp how wide and long and high and deep that love is—this love that surpasses knowledge. Bless me that I might increase in love as I exercise my hope in you. Today, I pray that I will hold firm to the love and Word of God, and draw my encouragement from it, that I may be filled to the measure of all the fullness of God.

—Adapted from Ephesians 3:16–21

# A Friend in Jesus

Lord, I am thankful every day that you sent your Son to live among us. How blessed we are that he taught us about you and gave us such a beautiful example to follow. May I remember every day to pause and give thanks for this, so I do not get too caught up in my trivial, worldly cares.

*What a friend we have in Jesus, all our sins and griefs to bear!*
—Joseph M. Scriven

# Count Your Blessings

If I count the things I've asked for that you have not given me, I begin to believe you do not love me, God. But if, instead, I bring to mind all of the goodness you have shown me, I come to trust that you have never given me less than what I need, and often have blessed me with far more, from a depth of love I cannot comprehend.

*There's so much to be grateful for in this life! Thank you, God, for your many blessings.*

# Ordinary Miracles

When we doubt your miracle-making power, Lord, show us the ordinary miracles of seasons, of hope regained, of love from family and friends, and of surprises that turn out to be miraculous simply by remaking our lives.

*To live in hope means to expect that our longings will be fulfilled. When we hold that image of fulfillment constantly, we cannot help but notice all the ways in which our lives are blessed.*

# Thank You

*Thank the Lord for his steadfast love, for his wonderful works to humankind.*
                                    Psalm 107:8

God, we thank you for this food,
   for the hands that planted it,
for the hands that tended it,
for the hands that harvested it,
for the hands that prepared it,
for the hands that provided it,
and for the hands that served it.
And we pray for those without enough
   food in your world and in our land
   of plenty.

*If the only prayer you say in your entire life is Thank you, that would suffice.*
                                    —Meister Eckhart

# Treasure of My Heart

*I give thanks to you, O Lord my God, with my whole heart, and I will glorify your name for ever.*

Psalm 86:12

Lord, you are the God who has set the foundations of the earth, who blessed Abraham with offspring "as numerous as the stars in heaven." You have blessed me, too, by giving me the treasure of my heart, my family. I pour out my thanks for this gift, which is far above any riches the world can give. How can I praise you enough?

Heavenly Father, I never fail to come to you for help and comfort in the dark times of my life, yet I don't always remember you when my cup is overflowing. Forgive me if I seem ungrateful and take your generosity for granted. How can I forget all that you give me each day?

You bring beauty, peace, and love to my existence. My heart overflows with thanksgiving.

> *Thou who has given so much to me, give one thing more: a grateful heart.*
> —George Herbert

# Grant Me Patience

*The Lord is good to those who wait for him, to the soul that seeks him. It is good that one should wait quietly for the salvation of the Lord.*

Lamentations 3:25–26

Waiting? Waiting is not my forte, Father. As someone who has a hard time waiting for the microwave to heat my lunch, waiting for your answers to prayer is sometimes excruciating. But I've come to see that these waiting periods are usually good for me. I grow in discipline, and I discover the peace of your presence.

# Joy of Living

Joyful, joyful, we adore Thee,
God of glory, Lord of love;
Hearts unfold like flowers before Thee,
Opening to the sun above.
Melt the clouds of sin and sadness;
Drive the dark of doubt away;
Giver of immortal gladness,
Fill us with the light of day!
Thou art giving and forgiving,
Ever blessing, ever blest,
Wellspring of the joy of living,
Ocean depth of happy rest!
Thou our Father, Christ our Brother,
All who live in love are Thine:
Teach us how to love each other,
Lift us to the joy divine.

—Henry van Dyke, "Hymn of Joy"

# Simple Things

*In every thing give thanks, for this is the will of God in Christ Jesus.*
1 Thessalonians 5:18 KJV

It sometimes takes a tragic event to open our eyes to the blessings that surround us, to show us the joy in life's simple moments. Day-to-day activities and events can seem mundane and repetitive until something happens that shakes our foundation and brings into sharp focus what is truly important and precious. Our family, friends, our neighbors, and our communities suddenly become havens of love, support, and comfort in the midst of tragedy.

Wise is the person who can see the magic and wonder in simple things without having to suffer a great loss or disaster. Happy is the person who knows that life's greatest treasures are often buried deep within the simplest things, waiting to be discovered by those who are paying attention.

*Savor the simple joys of life: the laughter of a child, a lazy Saturday morning, a surprise visit from a long-absent friend.*

# The Spirit Within

*Do you not know that you are God's temple
and that God's Spirit dwells in you?*

1 Corinthians 3:16

Imagine, if you can...
A love so deep it swallows fear,
A love so wide it embraces pain,
A love so high it humbles pride,
A love so thick it absorbs all sin.
Imagine, but don't stop there!
Come with your fear,
Your pain,
Your pride,
Your sin.
Come to God who loves—
Purely, perfectly, precisely—
You.

# The Lord's Delight

*The Lord thy God in the midst of thee is mighty; he will save, he will rejoice over thee with joy; he will rest in his love, he will joy over thee with singing.*
Zephaniah 3:17 KJV

O Lord, how I delight in knowing you and worshipping you—and how humbled I am to learn that you also delight in me! You created me to praise you, Lord, and I do so with a grateful heart. Thank you, Lord, for watching over me, loving me even when I don't deserve it, calming me, and rejoicing over me with singing. My heart will sing songs of gratitude to you each and every day of my life. Amen.

# Mosaic of Life

*The Lord will guide you continually,
and satisfy your needs.*

Isaiah 58:11

Guide me, O God, to savor today and all that is yet to be discovered. I know that what came before and what is yet to be form a marvelous mosaic of the whole.

*Look to this day,
For it is life,
The very life of life.
In its brief course lie all
The realities and verities of existence,
The bliss of growth,
The splendor of action,
The glory of power—
For yesterday is but a dream,
And tomorrow is only a vision,
But today, well lived,
Makes every yesterday a dream of
  happiness
And every tomorrow a vision of hope.*

—Sanskrit proverb

# Happy in God's Love

*Happy are those whose help is the God of Jacob, whose hope is in the Lord their God, who made heaven and earth, the sea, and all that is in them; who keeps faith for ever.*
Psalm 146:5–6

God, I feel happy today, and I have you to thank for that. No matter what is going on outside of me, I am strong and safe and secure inside because you love and care for me. Thank you for loving me when I have been cranky, tired, lazy, and even mean. Thank you for being there when I ignored your presence, God. Your steadfast love is a constant reminder of just how good I have it in life. And that makes me happiest of all!

# A Majestic God

*But the earth will be filled with the knowledge of the glory of the Lord, as the waters cover the sea.*

Habakkuk 2:14

Lord, how magnificent is your work on this earth. We can stand at the seashore and feel our own souls rising and filling with your majesty as we marvel at the tides. Or we can walk down a trail and notice that each and every twig has been frosted individually with more icy flakes than we can imagine. We praise you for this awesome creation you share with us, Lord. The more we see of it, the more amazed we are. To you be the glory!

# Longtime Friends

Longtime friendship is a two-way mirror, O God, a gift from you that returns our best selves reflected in the joy others get from just having us around. Thank you for the gift of perseverance that keeps old friendships new.

*May you be poor in misfortune, rich in blessings, slow to make enemies, quick to make friends. But rich or poor, quick or slow, may you know nothing but happiness from this day forward.*

—Traditional Irish blessing

# Count Your Blessings

Forgive me for complaining, dear God. Help me remember that every time I don't like the food in front of me, millions have nothing to eat; every time I think my paycheck is small, too many people have no paycheck at all; every time I wish my loved ones were not so demanding, some people have no one to love. Teach me perspective, God, and to be grateful for my gifts of family, food, and home.

*Count your blessings,*
  *name them one by one:*
*Count your blessings,*
  *see what God hath done.*
    —Johnson Oatman Jr.

# Change Is Good

Change is never easy, but the blessings it bestows upon us are magnificent. Just ask the caterpillar struggling within the tight confines of a cocoon. Even as it struggles, it is becoming something glorious, something beautiful, soon to emerge as a winged butterfly. Change may bring temporary pain and discomfort, but it also brings the promise of a new life filled with joy and freedom and the ability to soar even higher than we ever did before.

*All the great blessings of my life are present in my thoughts today.*
—Phoebe Cary

# God's Path

*You show me the path of life.*

Psalm 16:11

You hold in your hand my destiny. You determine, largely, whether I shall succeed or fail. Give me, I pray you, those things that make for happiness. Train me, I beg you, that I may be a blessing to the world.

—James L. Christensen, *New Ways to Worship*

# Showers of Blessing

*Blessed be his glorious name forever;
may his glory fill the whole earth.*

Psalm 72:19

Lord, I can hear your voice in the bubbling brook, see your beauty in the petals of a flower, and feel your gentle breath in the evening breeze and in the soft kiss of a child. Thank you for all of these gifts.

*There shall be showers of blessing,*
*This is the promise of love;*
*There shall be seasons refreshing,*
*Sent from the Saviour above.*

*Showers of blessing,*
*Showers of blessing we need;*
*Mercy drops round us are falling,*
*But for the showers we plead.*

*There shall be showers of blessing,*
*Precious reviving again;*
*Over the hills and the valleys*
*Sound of abundance of rain.*

—Major Daniel W. Whittle

# Rejoice in God

*Rejoice in the Lord always;
again I will say, Rejoice.*

Philippians 4:4

Lord, you are the source of all joy! Regardless of how happy we may feel at any given time, we know happiness is fleeting. Happiness, so dependent on temporary circumstances, is fickle and unpredictable. But joy in you is forever!

And so we come to you today, Lord, rejoicing in all you were, all you are, and all you will ever be. Because of you, we rejoice!

# Freedom from Worry

*Do not worry about anything, but in everything by prayer and supplication with thanksgiving let your requests be made known to God. And the peace of God, which surpasses all understanding, will guard your hearts and your minds in Christ Jesus.*

Philippians 4:6–7

Lord, even though I know worry is a waste of time and energy, it snares me again and again. Thank you for helping me notice early on that I'm about to wallow in worry once more. When I give my worry to you, Lord, I am able to find the blessings in the midst of all that's going on and thank you for them. I willingly trade my worry for your peace.

# True Joy

*Restore to me the joy of your salvation,
and sustain in me a willing spirit.*

Psalm 51:12

O Lord, I know it is from you and you only that I can receive pure joy. Don't let me miss the joy in today, Lord! Remind me of your glorious gift of salvation and keep my focus on you and your gifts to me. May I desire the joy that comes from finding you more meaningful than the fleeting happiness the world offers. In your name I pray, amen.

*Happiness comes and goes, but God's joy is constant and forever.*

# God's Dwellings

*As for me and my household,
we will serve the Lord.*

Joshua 24:15

Lord, what compassion you showered on your people when you grouped us into families! Thank you, Lord, for the homes we are privileged to enjoy. We are thankful for these sanctuaries for our children and grandchildren. May our homes and our families honor you, Lord, in all we say and do within them. Dwell with us, Lord. You are always welcome.

*Christ is the head of this house; the unseen guest in every room.*

—Anonymous

# God's Infinite Wisdom

*This also comes from the Lord of hosts; he is wonderful in counsel, and excellent in wisdom.*

Isaiah 28:29

Lord, I looked at a recent problem from every angle imaginable, but it wasn't until I filtered it through your Word that the gems of wisdom and understanding appeared. How lost we would be without your guidance, Lord, and how blessed we are to have your counsel.

# Blessing of Freedom

*For you were called to freedom, brothers and sisters; only do not use your freedom as an opportunity for self-indulgence.*

Galatians 5:13

I love the freedoms I enjoy as your child, Father. I also deeply appreciate the freedoms I enjoy as a citizen of a free country. Both citizenships—my heavenly one and my earthly one—call for responsible living on my part, but these responsibilities are really a joy and a privilege. Help me to always keep this in the forefront of my mind as I make choices each day.

# Marvelous Creations

*O Lord, our Sovereign, how majestic is your name in all the earth! You have set your glory above the heavens.*

Psalm 8:1

This morning I am marveling at the birds at the bird feeder, Lord. Those little creatures are so fascinating! Their plumage, the variety of sizes, shapes, beaks, tails, wings, calls…I feel a sense of pure delight at their existence. I can find so many things to be in awe of in this great, wide universe you have made. You have made it all to speak of your majesty—to tell us what you are like. I turn my heart toward heaven today, to worship and give glory to you, Lord.

# In Thanks for a Good Day

*I will praise the name of God with a song;*
*I will magnify him with thanksgiving.*

Psalm 69:30

How fortunate I feel today!
All is well.
Things are working out.
But is it luck…or is it your love?
I will assume the latter
and offer words of praise:
Bless your name, Almighty One!

# Spreading Light

*He said to them, "Is a lamp brought in to be put under the bushel basket, or under the bed, and not on the lampstand?"*

Mark 4:21

Thank you, God of inspiration, for the times when you guide me to stand tall as an example and a model for my family. For you call us to be loving, tender, and kind. Remind me that this call is more than just building a family, for the family is Christianity in miniature.

*There are two ways of spreading light: to be the candle or the mirror that reflects it.*

—Edith Wharton

# Breath of Life

*In his hand is the life of every living thing and the breath of every human being.*

Job 12:10

Lord, with each breath I take I am aware that it is you who breathed life into me. My next breath is as dependent on you as my last breath was. And I can confidently rest in the knowledge that it will be you and you alone who will determine when the last breath leaves my body and I go to be with you. Today, Lord, I thank you for the gift of life and for each breath I take.

# The Right Direction

*My God turns my darkness into light.*
Psalm 18:28 NIV

Dear Lord, thank you for always listening to my concerns. So often I begin praying in one direction, only to sense you turning my thoughts around until I end up praying for something quite different. Only later do I realize that you were gently guiding me in a better direction. What blessed communication! I am so grateful.

*When I pray and make contact with my Creator, I am inspired to live above the petty plateaus my soul has settled on, and I long to ascend into the heights of majestic mountains.*

# A Generous Spirit

*Those who are generous are blessed,
for they share their bread with the poor.*
                                    Proverbs 22:9

Sharing has to be one of life's most difficult lessons, O bountiful God. Remind me that to choose to "give away" my time, my energy, myself, makes a gracious gift instead of a grudging duty.

*Give what you have. To some it may be better than you dare think.*
—Henry Wadsworth Longfellow

# Present Blessings

May your thoughts focus much more upon what you have than what you lack in this trying time. May your heart lay hold of present realities rather than future possibilities. For this moment—the now—is all we are given. Whether we are sick or healthy, this juncture in time is the place we share. Let us be blessed in this moment, needing nothing to change. Let us simply be in God's presence, just for this moment.

*God's faithfulness blesses every part of our lives.*

# Mysterious Ways

*And this is the boldness we have in him, that if we ask anything according to his will, he hears us.*

1 John 5:14

God moves in a mysterious way,
His wonders to perform;
He plants his footsteps in the sea,
And rides upon the storm.
Deep in unfathomable mines
Of never-failing skill,
He treasures up his bright designs,
And works his sovereign will.
Ye fearful saints fresh courage take,
The clouds ye so much dread
Are big with mercy, and shall break
In blessings on your head.

—William Cowper,
"Light Shining Out of Darkness"

# *In Thanksgiving*

*O give thanks to the Lord, for he is good;*
*his steadfast love endures for ever!*

Psalm 118:1

We thank you, God, for the moments of fulfillment:
the end of a day's work,
the harvest of sugar cane,
the birth of a child,
for in these pauses we feel
the rhythm of the eternal.

—Hawaiian prayer

*We plow the fields and scatter
The good seed on the land,
But it is fed and watered
By God's almighty hand;
He sends the snow in winter,
The warmth to swell the grain,
The breezes and the sunshine,
And soft, refreshing rain.
All good gifts around us
Are sent from heaven above:
Then thank the Lord, O thank the Lord
For all His love.*

—Matthias Claudius

# True Friendship

A healthy friendship enhances our lives. What a blessing to have someone who wants to share all our joys and sorrows. We should continually strive to be the kind of friend God would like us to be—and the kind of friend we would like to have.

*A true friend is the greatest of all blessings.*
—Duc de La Rochefoucauld

# The Spirit at Work

*O Lord my God, I will give you thanks for ever.*

Psalm 30:12 NIV

Lord, so often it isn't until after a crisis has passed that we can see all the ways that you were present in the midst of it. Forgive us for focusing on the negative and missing your positive contributions. Remind us to expect your involvement—to actively watch for it, even! We need to be alert to the working of your Spirit in all things and give thanks at all times.

## Just Enough

Lord, how important it is for us to grasp the concept of "enough." You know how this world tempts us with all that is bigger, better—more in every way! But there is such joy and freedom in trusting that you will give us exactly what we need—neither too little nor too much. May we never take for granted all the blessings we have, Lord, and may we be as generous with others as you are with us. It is the simple life that brings us closest to you; we are blessed when we live simply.

*Find out how much God has given you and from it take what you need; the remainder is needed by others.*
—St. Augustine of Hippo

# All God's Creatures

*But ask the animals, and they will teach you; the birds of the air, and they will tell you.*

Job 12:7

Lord, how grateful I am that I once again notice the lovely animals all around me. There was a time in my life when I was so busy, I didn't see them at all, though I know they were always there. Now the birds, the deer—even the raccoons—bring me joy every day as I watch them from my window. Catching precious glimpses of these creatures of yours helps me value every moment of every day.

# Blessed Gathering

*There is nothing better for people under the sun than to eat, and drink, and enjoy themselves.*

Ecclesiastes 8:15

Lord, some of our best family times occur when we can all sit down together to enjoy a meal and conversation. After the blessing of food and family, everyone has a chance to be heard, humor is encouraged, and appetites flourish. Some of life's greatest problems are settled around our table. Father, I am grateful that you are a God who wants us to enjoy ourselves. I thank you for the food that you supply, the closeness of our family, and the circle of love that surrounds us.

# Provider for All

*Keep your lives free from the love of money, and be content with what you have; for he has said, "I will never leave you or forsake you."*

Hebrews 13:5

Father God, you are the giver of all gifts. All of our resources and all we have come from you, and they are only ours for a little while. Protect us from any addiction to material things, Lord. Gently remind us when we have enough—enough to eat, enough to wear, enough to enjoy. Most of all, keep us mindful of the fact that because we have you, we have everything we need.

# Precious Gifts

*The Lord upholds all who are falling, and raises up all who are bowed down.... You open your hand, satisfying the desire of every living thing. The Lord is just in all his ways, and kind in all his doings. The Lord is near to all who call on him, to all who call on him in truth.*

Psalm 145:16–18

O Lord, thank you for being a part of my work today. I can always tell when a thought or an idea comes from you because it's just too perfect to have been my own! That you care enough to be involved in my work is a precious gift to me, Lord—one I would never want to be without.

# God Is Love

*God is love, and those who abide in love abide in God, and God abides in them.*

1 John 4:16

Lord, your gift of love is often distorted in this world of ours. You are the source of the only perfect love we will ever know. Thank you, Lord, for abiding in us and helping us love ourselves and others. On this day, Lord, I pray that you will draw near to anyone who is feeling unloved. May they accept your unconditional love so they will know what true love is!

*God's love dwells in us and sustains us. It never disappoints.*

# Community of Faith

*O come, let us worship and bow down.*
Psalm 95:6

Lord, my heart is uplifted as I think of the gift you have given me: a community of faith. I thank you for my church and for the people who have become part of my support system. We need the blessings of church attendance. We need the fellowship and care of other believers; we need to be refreshed with the words of scripture and feel the power of prayer. We need to experience your presence, Lord, in your house and to become involved in your work.

*People—reaching out and reaching up—that is the church.*

# In Everything We Do

*For "In him we live and move and have our being.... For we too are his offspring."*
*Acts 17:28*

We thank you, Lord, who gave us sight and sense
to smell the flowers,
to hear the wind,
to feel the waters in our hand,
to sleep with the night and wake with the sun,
to stand upon this star,
to sing your praise,
to hear your voice.

*Blessed and praised be the Lord,*
*from whom comes all the good that*
*we speak and think and do.*
—St. Teresa of Avila

# Morning

God, you are so great. It is always the right time to worship you, but morning is best. Praise for the dawning light that streams in through this window. Praise for the sound of the birds as they flit through the air. Praise for the little spider crawling along on the ceiling. Praise for the smell of coffee and the warmth of a cup in my hands. Praise for the flowering plants—and even those weeds growing by the house. Praise for the neighbors walking along the sidewalk and the clouds moving by too. Most of all, praise for the breath that keeps flowing in and out of my lungs. Yes, this is the greatest item of praise: that you alone are my life—all life itself. Without you, all is dust. Praise...for you.

> *The true harvest of my daily life is somewhat as intangible and indescribable as the tints of morning or evening. It is a little star dust caught, a segment of the rainbow which I have clutched.*
> —Henry David Thoreau

# On the Blessings of Life

Go forth in the joy of the Lord, knowing how blessed you are. Celebrate the beauty of nature around you. Celebrate the goodness of fellowship with others. Celebrate the chance to take up the challenge of each day. Most of all: Celebrate your life. How blessed you are!

*May you be blessed*
   *with the strength of heaven—*
*the light of the sun and*
   *the radiance of the moon*
*the splendor of fire—*
*the speed of lightning—*
*the swiftness of wind—*
*the depth of the sea—*
*the stability of earth and*
   *the firmness of rock.*

—St. Patrick's breastplate

# Bless My Pets

God of beasts and critters, bless them, for they bless me even when they shed on the couch and don't come when called. They love without strings and share the simplest joys of walks and catnaps, slowing me to a pace you recommend.

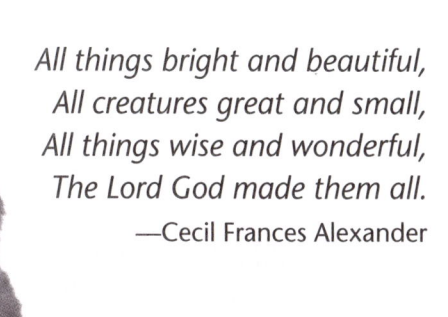

*All things bright and beautiful,*
*All creatures great and small,*
*All things wise and wonderful,*
*The Lord God made them all.*
—Cecil Frances Alexander

# Finding Rest

*Take my yoke upon you, and learn of me; for I am meek and lowly in heart: and ye shall find rest unto your souls.*

Matthew 11:29 KJV

Lord, how amazing it is that you are willing to come alongside me in everything I do. Doing things with you is abundantly easier than pulling the load all by myself. I know that, but then I take off in a new direction and forget that we are in this life together! Forgive me, Jesus, for I know that only when I stay close to you will my efforts produce anything worthwhile. Then, and only then, will I find true rest at the end of the day. Amen.

*Jesus, I am resting, resting
in the joy of what thou art;
I am finding out the greatness
of thy loving heart.*

*Thou hast bid me gaze upon thee;
and thy beauty fills my soul,
for by thy transforming power,
thou has made me whole.*

—Jean Sophia Pigott

# True Joy

*Although you have not seen [Jesus], you love him; and even though you do not see him now, you believe in him and rejoice with an indescribable and glorious joy.*

1 Peter 1:8

Jesus said that those who would believe in him without having seen him would be blessed. We get a glimpse of that blessing here in Peter's words of encouragement to the church. It is a blessing to live in such joy. People can work a lifetime to amass money and all the things it can buy without feeling such true joy. Yet those who trust in Christ have an abiding, "indescribable and glorious joy" that fills their innermost being.

# Gift of Laughter

*A cheerful heart is a good medicine,
but a downcast spirit dries up the bones.*
Proverbs 17:22

Lord, how we thank you for the gift of laughter! Even in the midst of grief you send those happy memories that make us laugh and bring comfort to our souls. Laughter is so healing, Lord. It's reassuring to see so much evidence of your sense of humor. I feel confident there will be lots of laughter in heaven!

# Goodness and Mercy

*Let us therefore approach the throne
of grace with boldness, so that we may
receive mercy and find grace
to help in time of need.*

Hebrews 4:16

The Lord hath spoken peace to
my soul,
He hath blessed me abundantly,
Hath pardoned my sins;
He hath shown me great mercy and
saved me by his love.

I will sing of His goodness and mercy
while I live,
And ever, forever will praise His
Holy name.

O how sweet to trust in God,
And to know your sins forgiven,
To believe His precious word,
And be guided by His love.

Therefore goodness and mercy,
Shall follow me all the days of my life.
Amen.

—C. E. Leslie

*The blessing of mercy is
the very heartbeat of God.*

# God's Creations

*When I look at your heavens, the work of your fingers, the moon and the stars that you have established; what are human beings that you are mindful of them, mortals that you care for them?*

Psalm 8:3–4

Lord, it's easy for us to get bogged down in the details of life. But when we have the opportunity to gaze at the stars on a clear night, it is easy to remember that there is more to your creation than our relatively insignificant lives. You placed the stars and know them by name, Lord, and you know us by name too. We are blessed to be a part of your magnificent creation! That you also care deeply for us is the best gift of all.

# Call Upon the Lord

*Seek the Lord while he may be found, call upon him while he is near.*

Isaiah 55:6

Lord, how incredible it is that we can connect with you without any of the technological trappings we think we need to communicate today. Our connection with you is heart to heart, and the lines of communication are open to all who turn to you in prayer with a contrite and willing spirit. Today I call upon you, Lord. Thank you for never failing to take my call.

*Prayer is still the best wireless connection available to us.*

# Older and Wiser

*The Lord blessed the latter days of Job more than his beginning.*

Job 42:12

Lord, I never imagined when I was young that growing older could be such a blessing. The experience and the wisdom I have now about how life works—these are gifts I would never trade for anything. Some people dread their later years, but mine are so blessed—I can only imagine how good the rest of my days will be. Thank you, Lord, for allowing me the privilege of getting older.

*The years teach much which the days never knew.*
—Ralph Waldo Emerson

# God's Word

*With my whole heart I seek you; do not let me stray from your commandments. I treasure your word in my heart, so that I may not sin against you.*

Psalm 119:10–11

Almighty God, how we thank you for providing your holy Word to guide and direct us, and how lost we would be without it! Whenever I open your Word, Lord, I hear you speaking words of encouragement and wisdom to me. I'm never the same when I close my Bible. Somehow seeing things as you see them gives me the clarity and direction I need for my day and for my life. Thank you, Lord, for your life-giving Word to us. Amen.

# Good Begets Good

*The world and its desire are
passing away, but those
who do the will of God live for ever.*

1 John 2:17

Help me take stock of your gifts to me, Lord. I'm good at things that appear to be so insignificant. Chances are you can use any one of them, no matter how simple it appears, to help others. Remind me that it's not what I do but my doing that ultimately matters.

*Gratitude is magnetic.
When you focus on the good in your life,
it tends to attract even more.*

# Simplify

Lord, I've stood by too many deathbeds to ever doubt that the adage "you can't take it with you" is absolutely true. We come into this world with nothing, and we leave with nothing. So why is it so tempting to spend so much of our lifetime striving for more money and possessions? We forget that all those things are fleeting and that the only people who are impressed by what we accumulate are those whose values are worldly. But you, O God, are eternal! Thank you for providing a way for us to be with you forever.

> *Our life is frittered away by detail...*
> *Simplicity, simplicity, simplicity.*
> —Henry David Thoreau

# Everyday Blessings

For the promise you unfold with
the opening of each day, I thank
you, Lord.
For blessings shared along the way,
I thank you, Lord.
For the comfort of our home filled with
love to keep us warm, I thank you, Lord.
For shelter from the winter storm,
I thank you, Lord.
For the gifts of peace and grace you
grant the family snug within,
I thank you, Lord.
For shielding us from harm and sin,
I thank you, Lord.
For the beauty of the snow sparkling in
the winter sun, I thank you, Lord.
For the peace when the day is done,
I thank you, Lord.

# True Friends

These Blessings, Reader,
  may Heav'n grant to thee;
A faithful Friend, equal in Love's degree;
Land fruitful, never conscious of the
  Curse,
A liberal Heart and never-failing Purse;
A smiling Conscience, a contented mind;
A temp'rate Knowledge with true
  Wisdom join'd;
A Life as long as fair, and when expir'd,
A kindly Death, unfear'd as undesir'd.

—Benjamin Franklin

*If life has introduced you
to even one person
you can call a true friend,
you are truly blessed.*

# Coming Home to God

*At that time I will bring you home, at the time when I gather you; for I will make you renowned and praised among all the peoples of the earth, when I restore your fortunes before your eyes, says the Lord.*

Zephaniah 3:20

God, the blessed feeling of being at home in your loving presence is like nothing else. The joy I feel when I know I never walk alone is the greatest of gifts, and when I look around at the wonderful people you have chosen to walk with me through life—my family and my friends— I truly know that I am loved. Thank you, God, for these miracles, these blessings, far too numerous to count. And to think I never have to look too far from home to find them is the best miracle of all.

*No greater blessing exists than the feeling of being where we belong, with the people who make us happy, in the homes that bring us comfort and a sense of peace, doing work that makes us feel needed and satisfied. When we find our "true north," we feel at home and blessings await us behind each and every door.*

# In the Moment

*Come no closer! Remove the sandals from your feet, for the place on which you are standing is holy ground.*

Exodus 3:5

Help us to relax, Lord of calming seas, so that we don't become numb to the joy and awe of life. For it's socially acceptable to kick off our shoes and tangibly feel the love. Make us alive, O God, to the holy grounds of life, and save us from taking these special places for granted.

*May your days be filled with moments of childlike awe and magic. May the wonder of life delight your heart and enchant your soul.*

# Blessing of Peace

*Let the peace of Christ rule in your hearts.*

Colossians 3:15

Lord, make me an instrument of your peace.
Where there is hatred, let me sow love;
Where there is injury, pardon;
Where there is doubt, faith;
Where there is despair, hope;
Where there is darkness, light;
And where there is sadness, joy.
O, Divine Master, grant that I may not so much seek to be consoled as to console;
To be understood as to understand;
To be loved as to love;
For it is in giving that we receive;
It is in pardoning that we are pardoned;
It is in dying that we are born to eternal life.

—St. Francis of Assisi

# Streams of Blessings

*For the Lord your God is bringing you into a good land, a land with flowing streams, with springs and underground waters welling up in valleys and hills,...a land where you may eat bread without scarcity, where you will lack nothing.*

Deuteronomy 8:7–9

Ever notice how the more grateful you are for the good things in your life, the more the floodgates tend to open, bringing even more good things? We lack for nothing when we are grateful for everything. That is when the blessings become a stream that never ceases to provide us with more to be grateful for.

# Merciful Love

*I will turn their mourning into gladness; I will give them comfort and joy instead of sorrow.*

Jeremiah 31:13 NIV

Precious Lord, bless me with your grace that I may experience the deepest peace and healing only you can provide. Show me the merciful love that knows no end, that I may rest today knowing I am cared for. Amen.

*The grace of the living God refreshes like cool, clear water on a hot day, giving my parched soul the sustenance and nourishment it needs.*

# Equally Precious

*Let your adornment be
the inner self with the lasting beauty
of a gentle and quiet spirit, which
is very precious in God's sight.*

1 Peter 3:4

Lord, sometimes I long to stand out. When I feel plain, help me to remember that I should be at work cultivating the gentle and quiet spirit that is precious to you. This type of spirit may not call out, "Here I am!" but it accomplishes much. I am doing what I can, and I leave the rest to you. I trust that you will bring all to fruition.

*All people are equally
precious in God's eyes.*

# Blessings of Fellowship

*I hope to spend some time with you,
if the Lord permits.*

1 Corinthians 16:7

Dear God, what joy we have in gathering to pray and praise you together. How encouraging it is to share what's happening on our separate life journeys and see your hand at work in so many different ways. Thank you for arranging those times of fellowship, Lord. They are blessed times indeed.

# Constant Love

*Blessed are the merciful,
for they will receive mercy.*

Matthew 5:7

Lord, your forgiveness, based in your love for me, has transformed my life. I've experienced inner healing and freedom in knowing that you have wiped my slate clean and made me your friend. Help me become an extension of your love to those around me. Let healing happen as I apply the salve of your forgiveness to the wounds others carry and to the wounds they inflict on me. Please strengthen me today while I carry it out in your name. Amen.

# Wise in God's Ways

*How you have counselled one who has no wisdom, and given much good advice!*

Job 26:3

Lord, so often I believe I know exactly what I think and why, but then I sense your gentle nudging to look at the situation from your perspective. How generous of you to shine your wisdom into the dark corners of my heart and mind! Make me a person wise in your ways—not one determined to have things my way.

*Integrity without knowledge is weak and useless, and knowledge without integrity is dangerous and dreadful.*

—Samuel Johnson

# Perpetual Blessings

*I will pour my spirit upon your descendants, and my blessing on your offspring. They shall spring up like a green tamarisk, like willows by flowing streams.*
Isaiah 44:3–4

Lord, it's hard to count your blessings when all around you is chaos and despair. Though my heart is heavy and my mind cluttered, please help me to realize that before a flower can show its beauty to the sun, it first is a seed buried in the dirt. Help me to stand above the negative things in life and cast my eyes instead upon the positives that are always there, like the seedling, growing toward the moment when it will appear above ground, face to the sun.

# Celebrate Life

God, help me celebrate this day with all my heart, to rejoice in the beauty of its light and warmth. May I give thanks for the air and grass and sidewalks. Help me feel grateful as others flow into my soul. May I cherish the chance to work and play, to think and speak—knowing this: All simple pleasures are opportunities for praise.

*So much to celebrate! Waking to dawn gilding trees; squeezing fresh orange juice, its zest clinging to my hands all day; making a new friend, talking to an old one; watching the first leaf bud, raking the last. Each day's turning brings gifts to celebrate.*

# Sing for Joy

*Come, let us sing for joy to the Lord; let us shout aloud to the Rock of our salvation. Let us come before him with thanksgiving and extol him with music and song. For the Lord is the great God, the great King above all gods. In his hand are the depths of the earth.*

Psalm 95:1–4 NIV

Go forth in the joy of the Lord, knowing how blessed you are.

# Meeting God in the Garden

*You shall be like a watered garden, like a spring of water, whose waters never fail.*
Isaiah 58:11

Almighty God, how I love seeing your handiwork in the garden. The intricacy of each petal that blooms, the whimsy of the ladybug, and even the dedicated work of the lowly earthworm all testify to the glory of your creation. Whether I'm working the soil, planting, pulling weeds, or simply relaxing there, being in the garden restores my soul, Lord. I can only believe that's because you choose to meet me there so we can enjoy your creation together. Thank you, Lord. Amen.

*I come to the garden alone,*
*While the dew is still on the roses;*
*And the voice I hear, falling on my ear,*
*The Son of God discloses.*
*And He walks with me,*
*And He talks with me,*
*And He tells me I am His own;*
*And the joy we share as we tarry there*
*None other has ever known.*

—C. Austin Miles

# God's Children

*Then little children were being brought to him in order that he might lay his hands on them and pray.*

Matthew 19:13

Lord, what a blessing children are in this world. They bring such joy into our lives and are a precious composite of the best of our past and the hopes for the future. Thank you for your love for all children, Lord. Please guard them always.

*The laughter of a child is the light of a house.*
—African proverb

# A Generous God

*If any of you is lacking in wisdom, ask God, who gives to all generously and ungrudgingly, and it will be given you.*

James 1:5

Well, Lord, since you're offering, I'm not going to be shy about asking. I need wisdom. I need it today as I'm dealing with people and situations and wondering what the best approach or decision might be. Thank you for being generous with your gifts rather than giving them to only a select few. In fact, you make receiving them as simple as just asking. You never cease to amaze me with your generosity, Lord. I'm deeply grateful.

# Good Fruit

*I am the vine, you are the branches.
Those who abide in me and I in them bear
much fruit, because apart from me
you can do nothing.*

John 15:5

Lord, please help me to remember that you are the source of all good things that come out of my life as I grow and flourish in you. All the "good fruit" of love, joy, peace, patience, kindness, goodness, faithfulness, gentleness, and self-control come directly from you and then produce good things in me. I want to thank you for nourishing and supporting my life. Please use the fruit you're producing in me to nourish others and lead them to you as well.

# For Family

Loving God,
bless our family with your love.
Guard us from all danger and harm;
deliver us from anger that leads
   to division;
empower us to forgive as we have
   been forgiven;
and send us into the world to witness
   your love and grace;
in the name of Jesus Christ we pray.
Amen.

—Vienna Cobb Anderson

*Bless all that happens here, O God. May we find laughter and love and strength and sanctuary. Bless all who visit our love-built home. May we, like you, offer shelter and welcome.*

# A Blessing of Healing

*Come, let us return to the Lord; for it is he who has torn, and he will heal us.*

Hosea 6:1

Lord, the only blessing I ask for these days is to restore my body to good health. When I am healthy and strong, everything else seems easier and I have the fortitude to handle challenges that come my way. Bless me with good health and vitality, and help me treat my body right and avoid stress when I can.

*A wise man should consider that health is the greatest of human blessings, and learn how by his own thought to derive benefit from his illnesses.*

—Hippocrates

# Generous God

*I will send down the showers in their season; they shall be showers of blessing.*
Ezekiel 34:26

Lord, my heart overflows with gratitude for all the blessings you have sent into my life. I am cognizant of the fact that I am probably only aware of a small percentage of them, though. You are such a generous God; you shower us with such abundance. I am grateful for it all, Lord.

# Real Wealth

The world holds so many priceless things—the falling rain, a rose in bloom, the wind that sings, an oyster's pearl, the mustard seed. If we can cherish just one precious gift, our lives will be rich indeed.

*Do not depend too much upon your own industry, and frugality, and prudence, though excellent things, for they may all be blasted without the blessing of Heaven; and therefore, ask that blessing humbly, and be not uncharitable to those that at present seem to [lack] it, but comfort and help them. Remember, Job suffered, and was afterwards prosperous.*

—Benjamin Franklin

# Extreme Love

*In this was manifested the love of God toward us, because that God sent his only begotten Son into the world, that we might live through him.*

1 John 4:9 KJV

You are everywhere, Lord, and I'm comforted to be enfolded as I move through life's extremes. You are with me in birthings and dyings, in routine and surprise, and in stillness and activity. I cannot wander so far in any direction that you are not already there.

*With his presence, his word, and his people, God comforts us.*

# Friendship and Love Intertwined

God, encouragement through friends and family lifts my heart just as sunshine turns roses skyward. May their love inspire me to stretch my soul toward the warmth and nurture of your radiant affection for me.

*The thread of our life would be dark, heaven knows, if it were not with friendship and love intertwined.*
—Sir Thomas Moore, *Friendship Is a Special Gift*

# Every Day's a Blessing

*In your book were written all
the days that were formed for me, when
none of them as yet existed.*

Psalm 139:16

Lord, how I love to wake up to a cool, crisp fall day with snowcapped mountains in the distance and the blue sky above. On mornings like this I think, "What a wonderful day to be alive!" I soon realize, however, that I should see each day of my life as an extraordinary gift. Help me remember to value each day, Lord. And may I find in each of them a way to bring glory to you.

# Sound Sleepers

*And you will have confidence, because there is hope; you will be protected and take your rest in safety.*

Job 11:18

Security, loving God, is going to sleep in the assurance that you know my heart before I speak and are waiting, as soon as you hear from me, to transform my concerns into hope and action, my loneliness into companionship, and my despair into dance.

*Unseen, yet felt on the face like a summer breeze, faith lifts and supports, filling spirits with assurance.*

# Encourage One Another

*Therefore encourage one another and build up each other, as indeed you are doing.*
1 Thessalonians 5:11

God, a call, a note, and a handclasp from a friend are simple and seemingly insignificant. Yet you inspire these gifts from people we have a special affection for. These cherished acts of friendship nudge aside doubts about who we are when we feel low and encourage our hearts in a way that lifts our spirits. Thank you for the friends you have given us.

# Life's Rewards

*Hannah prayed and said, "My heart exults in the Lord; my strength is exalted in my God.... I rejoice in my victory."*

1 Samuel 2:1

Victories—both big and small—are sweet when they come from you, God. Promotions, honors, breakthroughs, discoveries, answered prayers...it's fun to savor them and know that your gracious hand has provided them. Help me remember to thank you when I taste victory today and to give you praise in all circumstances. My greatest reward in this life is your abiding presence with me.

# Spiritual Wealth

*Happy are those who find wisdom,*
*and those who get understanding,*
*for her income is better than silver,*
*and her revenue better than gold.*

Proverbs 3:13–14

Lord, you know how much time and effort I put into surrounding myself with my favorite things. Sometimes I wonder if it's always worth it. Please help me sort out what's truly valuable and what I can do without. One thing that I know is worth pursuing is the wisdom found in your Word. As I read it and your Spirit helps me to comprehend it, I feel rich indeed.

# Unequaled Peace

*L*ift up your heart in sweet surrender to the God who is waiting to shower you with blessings. Lift up your soul on wings of joy to the God who is waiting to guide you from the chaos of shadows out into the light of a peace that knows no equal.

*Deep peace of the running waves to you.*
*Deep peace of the flowing air to you.*
*Deep peace of the smiling stars to you.*
*Deep peace of the quiet earth to you.*
*Deep peace of the watching*
   *shepherds to you.*
*Deep peace of the Son of Peace to you.*

—Gaelic prayer

# God's View

*With us is the Lord our God to help us, and to fight our battles.*

2 Chronicles 32:8 KJV

Here we are again, Lord. Another time when I feel as if I've made a complete mess of this life you've given me. I place myself in your hands. If you need to totally reshape me to turn me into someone more useful, so be it! Thank you for not abandoning me, your humble creation. Make me over in your design.

*Faith in God's love frees me to be the real me, for I remember that God sees me as I am and loves me with all his heart.*

# Opportunities Abound

All our opportunities, abilities, and resources come from God. They are given to us to hold in sacred trust for him. Cooperating with God will permit us to generously pass on to others some of the many blessings from his rich storehouse.

*If I choose to act on even one opportunity to do good, I will have introduced a new blessing into my world.*

# A Mother's Love

*Mary treasured all these words and pondered them in her heart.*

Luke 2:19

What a wonderful, loving mother Mary was! As she listened to the amazing things people had to say about her child, Mary listened, pondering these things and filing them away in her heart. May all mothers look to Mary's example, Lord. May we parent generously and wisely, gently encouraging our children to look to your plans for their lives.

*What are Raphael's Madonnas but the shadow of a mother's love, fixed in permanent outline forever?*
—Thomas Wentworth Higginson

# Light of the World

*I am the light of the world. Whoever follows me will never walk in darkness but will have the light of life.*

John 8:12

Be thou my vision, O Lord of my heart;
Naught be all else to me, save that thou art:
Thou my best thought, by day or by night,
Walking or sleeping, thy presence my light.
Riches I heed not, or man's empty praise,
Thou mine inheritance, now and always:
Thou and thou only, first in my heart,
High King of heaven, my treasure thou art.

—Mary Byrne, "Be Thou My Vision"

*Jesus is the Light of the world. Living near him is the brightest place in the universe. To find out where he lives, read the Gospels and follow his path.*

—John Piper, *Hunger for God*

# Full of Spirit

*I am about to do a new thing;*
*now it springs forth, do you not perceive*
*it? I will make a way in the wilderness*
*and rivers in the desert.*

Isaiah 43:19

God, I thank thee for the gift of another day.
May I meet the unspent hours that are ahead
With brave heart as one who puts his trust in thee
And trusting is unafraid.
May every thought be pure and every purpose holy.
Make me generous in spirit, tolerant in judgment,

Unselfish in all human relations.
Keep back the hasty or the careless
 words,
And may nothing that I do or say wound
 or harm another.
May I meet life courageously,
Bearing with patience the hope deferred
And the dream unrealized.
—Alfred Grant Walton

*Ask, knock, search—imperative verbs implying God's blessing on our quests.*

# Unity in Love

*How very good and pleasant it is when kindred live together in unity!*

Psalm 133:1

Lord, behold our family here assembled. We thank Thee for this place in which we dwell; for the love that unites us; for the peace accorded us this day; for the hope with which we expect the morrow; for the health, the work, the food, and the bright skies, that make our lives delightful; for our friends in all parts of the earth.

—Robert Louis Stevenson

# In Remembrance

*Pay to all what is due them—taxes to whom taxes are due, revenue to whom revenue is due, respect to whom respect is due, honour to whom honour is due.*

Romans 13:7

Lord, you have told us to "remember the days of old." Memorials have played a large part in the history of your people in Israel, and we thank you for these reminders to honor the past. In giving honor to others, we thank and honor you, O God, for your love and for the great sacrifice of your son, Jesus Christ.

*To honor our past is to enrich our future.*

# Walk the Talk

*For he held fast to the Lord; he did not depart from following him but kept the commandments that the Lord commanded Moses. The Lord was with him; wherever he went, he prospered.*

2 Kings 18:6–7

God, there are so many times throughout my day when my words don't match my actions. I know others are looking to me to be an example of living rightly, but sometimes I just need help keeping my integrity. Help me to not break promises, to watch what I commit to—or overcommit to—especially if I know in my heart I cannot come through. Most of all, match my outer actions to my inner thoughts so that I am walking the talk. I get frustrated when others don't come through with their promises, and I ask that you help me to not become one of those people myself.

*Prosperous blessings await those who live rightly and keep their promises, just as God keeps promises made to us. Integrity is a powerful activator of blessings and miracles. When we talk the talk and walk the walk, and keep our eyes on the higher prize, we will never fail to find miracles waiting for us around every corner.*

# God's Grace

*The Lord, your God, is in your midst, a warrior who gives victory;*
*he will rejoice over you with gladness, he will renew you in his love.*

Zephaniah 3:17

Heavenly Father, your grace can refresh and renew me with the living water of hope and faith. Help me fully live the life you have given me. Amen.

*Amazing grace! How sweet the sound*
*that saved a wretch like me!*
*I once was lost, but now am found;*
*was blind, but now I see.*

*The Lord has promised good to me,*
*his word my hope secures;*
*he will my shield and portion be,*
*as long as life endures.*
—John Newton, "Amazing Grace"

# Relinquishing Control

*And now, our God, we give thanks to you and praise your glorious name.*

1 Chronicles 29:13

Lord, how important it is for us to be thankful at all times. It's so easy to fall into the trap of having specific expectations and then despairing when events take an unexpected turn. You are working in our lives every moment, Lord. We will do our part by working hard and taking full advantage of all opportunities that come our way, but we also know that some matters are reserved for you. We are thankful that nothing is beyond your control, Lord, and we are grateful that you are our wise leader.

# For One Who Lives Well

Blessed are you who know how to celebrate the goodness of life. Blessed because you choose to see the grace above and beyond the pain. Blessed because you see a potential friend in every stranger you meet. Blessed because you know the darkest clouds have brilliant silver linings. And most blessed because: All you ever knew of the half-empty glass was that it was almost full.

*Blessings brighten when we count them.*
—Maltbie D. Babcock

# Helping Each Other

Father, help us to touch and influence others. We want them to recognize and celebrate even the small blessings. We want to surprise them with gestures of love. Amen.

*Time binds words, bones,*
*And those who work together.*
*Time bends meanings, mountain spines,*
*    and daylight.*
*Time braids our calamity and joy,*
*Melts together our many moods,*
*Strains them and serves up to God the*
*    resulting libation;*
*Sweet or sour—strong or weak.*
*Time will take us*
*From this measured dimension*
*And deliver us to eternity.*
*Blessed are those who help along the way.*

# Angels on Earth

Dear Lord, I am blessed to have such good friends in my life, friends who share my sadness and my joy, my pain and my excitement, and who are always there for me when I need them. Just as I can lean on you for anything, Lord, I know you have given me these angels on earth who I can lean on as well. The love of these wonderful people fills my soul. I could not imagine living without them. May I always do for them what they have done for me.

*Blessings often come in the form of people God has chosen to bring into our lives. Some will be teachers, and some will be angels. Some will be both. Those we call our friends.*

# Miracles Abound

*The Lord has done great things for us.*
Psalm 126:3

Lord, how good have you been to me? Let me count the ways! In times of discouragement all I need to do is remember all the times you stepped in to set wrongs right, gave me a second chance, or showed up with a last-minute miracle. Lord, you are so good. May my faith never waver.

*All is a miracle. The stupendous order of nature, the revolution of a hundred million worlds around a million stars, the activity of light, the life of all animals, all are grand and perpetual miracles.*
—Voltaire

# Heaven's Blessings

Follow God's ways and be set free to live a life full of heavenly blessings.
Count neither the hours nor the seconds
That filled your mind with doubts and fears.
Do not add up unhappy moments,
When pain and hardships brought you to tears.
Regard not days on faded calendars
That marked the passage of your years.
Instead, count heaven's blessings…

Grandchildren playing on the floor,
Old friends walking through the door,
White clouds drifting up above,
And, like a faithful timepiece, God's love.

# Miracle of Life

*I praise you, for I am fearfully and wonderfully made. Wonderful are your works; that I know very well.*

Psalm 139:14

Lord, what a miracle each newborn baby is. We marvel at the tiny hands and rosebud lips, and we know such a masterpiece could only come from you! We pray for all little children today, Lord. Watch over them and guide their parents. Grant all parents the courage, strength, and wisdom they need to fulfill their sacred duties.

# Blessing of Wisdom

Blessings upon you. The blessing of perfect acceptance in the face of daunting circumstances. The blessing of contentment and peace while the winds blow and the waves rise higher.

Blessings upon you. The blessing of knowing when acceptance must turn to action for the sake of all concerned. The blessing of strength to forsake contentment and peace for the purpose of comforting another.

Blessings upon you. The blessing of discernment: to recognize when to wait and to understand when to move.

*God's Spirit offers us the blessing of inner peace.*

# Hand of God

*Humble yourselves therefore under the mighty hand of God, so that he may exalt you in due time. Cast all your anxiety on him, because he cares for you.*

1 Peter 5:6–7

Lord, I open my eyes and all I see are the amazing blessings that surround me. In this moment, I want for nothing, and I live with the knowledge that I can always turn to you for help, and cast my cares upon you, when my clarity and my vision cloud with worry. Thank you, Lord, for reminding me that the joyful blessings of this moment are all because of your love for me.

*The blessings of life, both small and big, are impossible to recognize when your heart is filled with worry and your eyes are on everything but the present. Remember, in the present is where the gift awaits.*

# Author of Love

*[Jesus said] "You shall love the Lord your God with all your heart, and with all your soul, and with all your mind." This is the greatest and first commandment. And a second is like it: "You shall love your neighbor as yourself."*

Matthew 22:37–39

Heavenly Father, you are the author of love. We are able to love only because you first loved us. You taught us how to love you and each other—our family and our neighbors. We want everyone to know your perfect love, and we invite the fragrance of your love to permeate our homes.

# Lovable Differences

Bless our differences, O Lord. And let us love across all barriers, the walls we build of color, culture, and language. Let us turn our eyes upward and remember: The God who made us all lives and breathes and moves within us, untouched by our petty distinctions. Let us love him as he is, for he loves us just as we are.

*God passes through the thicket of the world, and wherever his glance falls he turns all things to beauty.*

—St. John of the Cross

# Worthy of Love

Not everyone has the special family that I have, nor do they have the extra opportunities to open their hearts in the way my family does. We are not limited by what the neighbors think nor by society's current popular prejudices. We are far more than that. We are a family that comes from love, and we accept with pride every unique member. We are all special, and we are all worthy of love. I love and accept each member of my wonderful family, and they in turn love and adore me.... We are safe, and all is well in our world.

—Louise L. Hay

*A happy family is but an earlier heaven.*
—Sir John Bowring

# God's Artistry

*He has made everything
beautiful in its time.*

Ecclesiastes 3:11 NIV

God of all creation, I thank you for the beauty of the earth. Every leaf, every grain of sand, sings of your love. Each creature reveals your unique artistry. The sun and stars witness to your greatness.

You have woven together a natural world full of surprises for us to enjoy and mysteries for us to solve, and you have made us the stewards of this vast treasury. Thank you for your confidence in us.

**Acknowledgments:**

"God give me joy" Copyright © 1930 by *The Christian Century*. "God give me joy" by Thomas Curtis Clark is reprinted by permission from the August 6, 1930, issue of *The Christian Century*.

Excerpt from *Life Is What You Make It* by Alfred Grant Walton. Used by permission of Fleming H. Revell, a division of Baker Book House Company. Copyright © 1942.

Excerpt from *New Ways to Worship* by James L. Christensen. Used by permission of Fleming H. Revell, a division of Baker Book House Company. Copyright © 1973.

Excerpt from *Prayers of Our Hearts in Word and Action* by Vienna Cobb Anderson. Copyright © 1991. Used by permission of Vienna Cobb Anderson.

Unless otherwise noted, all scripture quotations are taken from the *New Revised Standard Version* of the Bible. Copyright © 1989 National Council of the Churches of Christ in the United States of America. Used by permission. All rights reserved.

Scripture quotations marked NIV are taken from *The Holy Bible, New International Version*®, NIV®. Copyright © 1973, 1978, 1984 by Biblica, Inc.™ Used by permission of Zondervan. All rights reserved worldwide. www.zondervan.com

Scripture quotations marked KJV are taken from *The Holy Bible, King James Version*.